The Usborne Nature Trail Book of
WILD FLOWERS

Written by Sue Tarsky and Margaret Stephens
Series Editor Sue Jacquemier
Consultant Editors Sally Heathcote, B.Sc., Jean Mellanby
Editorial revision by Margaret Stephens
Designed by Nick Eddison
Design revision by Amanda Barlow

Illustrated by
Andrew Beckett, Graham Austin,
Roger Kent, Gillian Platt (The Garden Studio),
Charles Raymond (Virgil Pomfret Agency),
David Ashby, David Baxter, Hilary Burn,
Liz Butler, Patrick Cox, Victoria Gordon, Colin King,
Deborah King, David Nash, Gwen Simpson,
George Thompson, Joan Thompson, Joyce Tuhill,
Phil Weare, Isabelle Bowring.

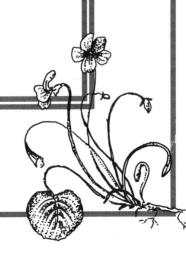

This book is full of the most
common flowers you can find in
the countryside, cities and towns
of Europe. Wherever you are, up
a mountain or on the seashore,
walking in a city car park or along
a river bank, you will find flowers.
If you want to identify them then
take this book with you and turn
to the pages which deal with the
kind of place you are in. If that
fails then turn to the pages that list
flowers by their colour and see if
you can find the correct pictures
there.

As well as helping you to
identify different flowers, this
book tells you how plants live,
how they grow and how their
seeds are scattered.

If you have enjoyed reading and
learning about flowers, then on
the last page there is a list of clubs
and books to help you continue
your studies.

Foxglove

**Wood
Anemone**

Marsh Marigold

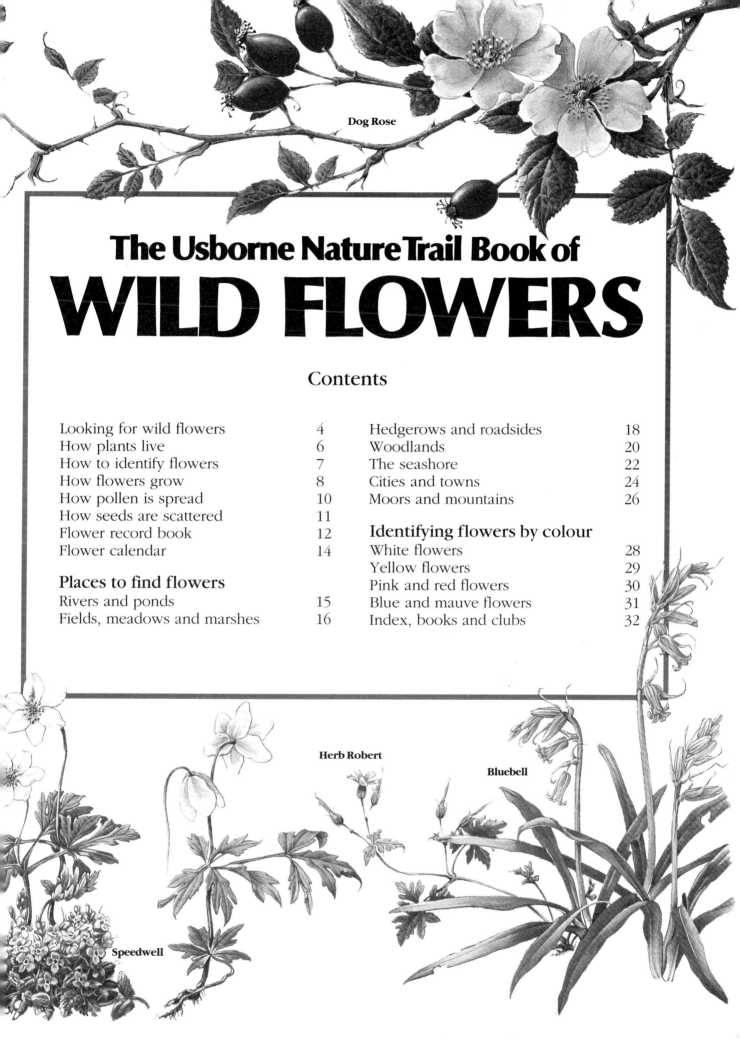

Dog Rose

The Usborne Nature Trail Book of
WILD FLOWERS

Contents

Herb Robert

Bluebell

Speedwell

Looking for wild flowers

When you go looking for wild flowers, take a notebook with you and two pencils for making notes and quick sketches. A tape measure, magnifying glass and outdoor thermometer are useful too. Record all you can about a flower, such as its height, colour and where it is growing. Use the magnifying glass to study the small parts.

Never dig up flowers and only pick them if you are sure they are common and there are lots of the same kind growing together. Take sheets of blotting paper to press them.

This is what the inside of a buttercup looks like. Other flowers may look different. Try to draw what you see inside the flower you have found.

JULY 12th 1991
STOUR MEADOWS 20°C

flowers are yellow

flower heads are 20mm across

flowers are flat on top

flowers look like a daisy

Plant has hairs

leaves are oval and pointed at ends

Plant is 40cm high

leaves have wavy edges

Stamens

Petal

Stigma

Ovary

Sepal

Magnifying glass

Thermometer

Tape measure

4

are flowers

e three flowers shown on the right
e very rare indeed. If you think you
ay have found a rare flower, do not
ck it. If you do, the flower will
come even more rare and it may
appear completely from the spot
here you found it.

nstead, make a careful drawing of the
wer and record in your notebook
actly where you found it. Show these
an adult who knows about rare
wers. If it is rare, you can report it to
conservation or nature club.

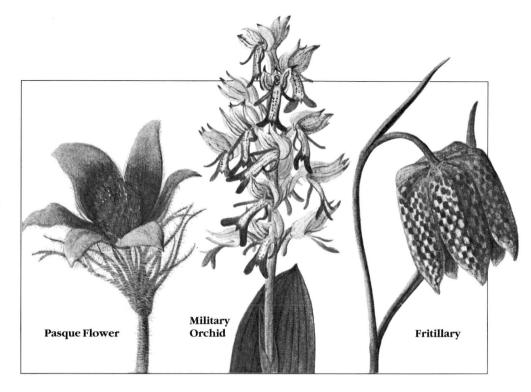

Pasque Flower   **Military Orchid**   **Fritillary**

How to make a flower map

The easiest way to make a map is to draw it as you walk along a route you know well. Draw lines for a road or path and make them turn in the same way you do.

Put in symbols for bridges, buildings and other special places. Wherever you find wild flowers, mark the place with a star. Use different colour stars for different types of flowers. Draw the symbols on the bottom of your map and write down next to them what they mean, so that everyone can understand them.

If you like, you can use a scale to show distance. Then anyone looking at it can understand how far apart everything is.

You can choose any scale you want. This map has a scale of 2 cm for every 50 paces.

SYMBOLS FOR YOUR MAP

 FLOWERS
 WOODS
STREAM
 GRASSLAND
HILLS
 MARSHES, WATER
 BRIDGE
 HOUSES

How plants live

The Rosebay Willowherb and the Field Buttercup have flowers with petals and sepals. They also have leaves, stems and roots. Most other plants have the same parts, but they can be different shapes and sizes.

Each part of a plant does one special thing that helps the plant to live. Leaves make food for a plant. During the day, they take in a gas from the air called carbon dioxide. This gas, the green colouring in the leaves, water and sunlight are used by the leaves to make food.

Leaves breathe out gases and water and take in gases from the air through tiny holes, so small you cannot see them with a magnifying glass.

Rosebay Willowherb

The **flower** is a very important part of the plant. It is here that the seeds grow.

The **sepals** protect the flower when it is in bud. When the flower is open, they lie underneath the petals. All the sepals together are called the calyx.

The **petals** may be brightly coloured o scented to attract insects. Some flow need insects to car pollen to other flow for pollination (see page 10), so the brighter the colour the more insects th flower will attract.

Field Buttercup

The **leaves** make food and "breathe" for the plant. They also get rid of any water that the plant does not need. Because leaves need light to make food, the whole plant grows towards light. Some plants close their leaves at night.

The **stem** carries water from the roots to the leaves, and carries food made in the leaves to the rest of the plant. It also holds the leaves up to the light.

The **roots** hold the plant firmly in the ground and draw up water from the soil that the plant needs.

How to identify flowers

Colour and place

When trying to identify a flower the first thing you notice is colour. The shape of its petals, sepals and leaves and the place where you found it are useful also.

Columbine
The Columbine has a blue or dark violet colour. The flower grows in open woods and lowlands.

Bloody Cranesbill
The flowers are a bright purplish crimson and grow in dry, grassy places.

Bluebell
Bluebells are usually blue, but can sometimes be white. They grow in woods and in many grassy areas.

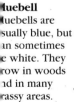

Flowers and stems

One flower on one stem

Small flowers in bunches

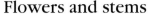

Primrose   **Cow Parsley**

Plants can have one flower on one stem, or many small flowers bunched together.

Petals

Scarlet Pimpernel   Foxglove

Petals joined together

Petals separate

A flower's petals may not all be the same shape and size, and they can be joined together or separate.

Sepals

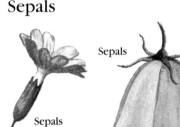

Sepals

Sepals

Red Campion

Harebell

Sepals can be many different shapes and sizes, and can be joined together or separate.

Mouse-ear Hawkweed
The flowers are lemon-yellow. They grow in most places where there is short grass.

Leaves

Wood Anemone

Leaf divides into three parts, joined at the base.

Leaves can be single, as in the Bugle (below). They can also be in separate parts. The Wood Anemone (above) has leaves which divide into three parts joined at the base. Sometimes the parts are on little stalks. These are called leaflets.

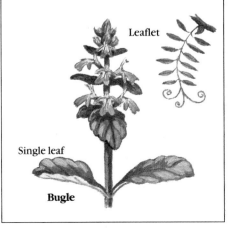

Leaflet

Single leaf

Bugle

How flowers grow

Almost every plant has a male part, called the stamen, and a female part, called the pistil. The Common Poppy has a group of stamens in the centre of the flower which grow around the pistil (see picture 3).

These pages tell you how the stamens and the pistil in a poppy work together to make seeds and how insects, such as bees, play a very important part by carrying pollen from flower to flower. These seeds will leave the plant and become new plants. Not all plants make seeds in this way, but many do.

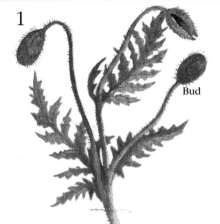

1

In the spring, the new plant grows from a seed buried in the ground. Later, many buds will develop on the plant.

Bud

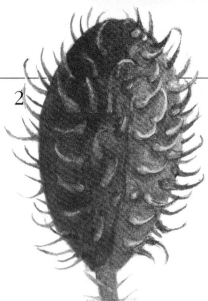

2

The sepals protect the flower when it is inside the bud. As the flower grows, the sepals begin to open.

6 When a bee visits another poppy some of this pollen may fall off onto the other flower's stigma. This is called pollination.

When the pollen grains land on top of the stigma, very thin tubes begin to grow down towards the ovary.

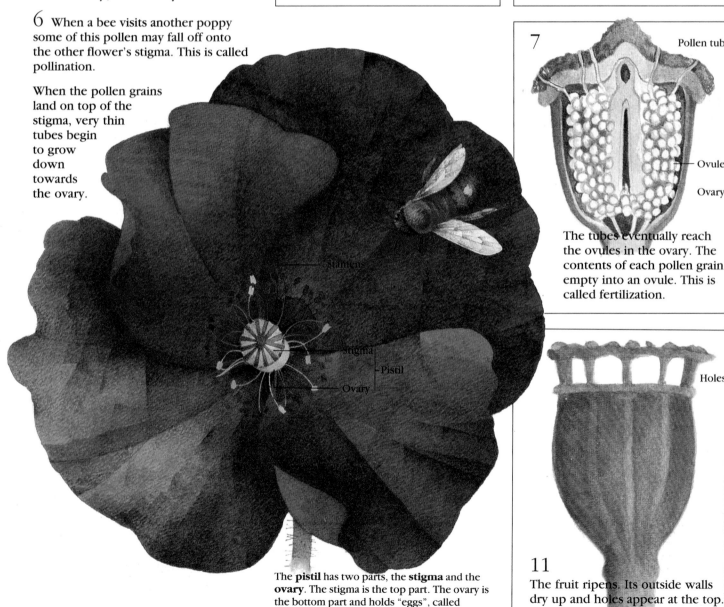

Stamens

Stigma

Pistil

Ovary

The **pistil** has two parts, the **stigma** and the **ovary**. The stigma is the top part. The ovary is the bottom part and holds "eggs", called ovules.

7

Pollen tube

Ovule

Ovary

The tubes eventually reach the ovules in the ovary. The contents of each pollen grain empty into an ovule. This is called fertilization.

Holes

11

The fruit ripens. Its outside walls dry up and holes appear at the top.

3
In the summer, the petals open. You can see the stamens (the male parts) and the pistil (the female parts).

Pollen

Anther

4
The small sacs at the end of the stamens, called anthers, open. The powder they hold, called pollen, escapes.

5
When a bee visits a poppy to feed, pollen from the stamens sticks to its hairy body or onto its legs.

Pollen

8
Once fertilization has taken place, the pollen on the stamens falls off and the stamens and petals wilt.

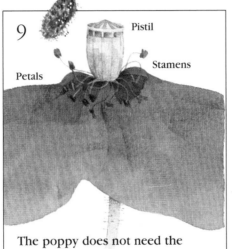

Pistil

Stamens

Petals

9
The poppy does not need the stamens or the petals any more and they fall off. But the pistil is still needed. It remains strong.

Fruit

10
Inside the pistil, the fertilized ovules are growing to form seeds. They are attached to the inside walls of the ovary. At this stage the ovary is called fruit.

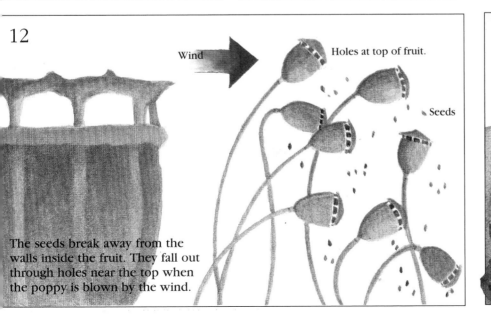

Wind

Holes at top of fruit.

Seeds

12
The seeds break away from the walls inside the fruit. They fall out through holes near the top when the poppy is blown by the wind.

13 The seeds which fall out of the fruit onto the soil in the autumn may grow into new plants the next spring.

How pollen is spread

In most plants, pollen must travel to another plant of the same sort to make seeds in an ovary. The pollen from a Common Poppy plant can only make seeds in another Common Poppy plant, not the one it came from (see pages 8-9). This is called cross-pollination.

In a few plants, such as the Red Helleborine on this page, pollen can make seeds grow in an ovary from the same flower. This is called self-pollination. Pollen can never make seeds grow in another sort of plant. Pollen from a rose cannot pollinate a daisy.

Insects feed on the nectar inside flowers and they can carry pollen from plant to plant when it sticks to their bodies. The colour of petals or scent can attract insects into the flowers. Some flowers have spots or lines on their petals called nectar guides. The insects follow these guides to find nectar.

The wind carries pollen too and in the summer the air is full of it. It can give people hayfever and make them sneeze.

By insects

Daisy

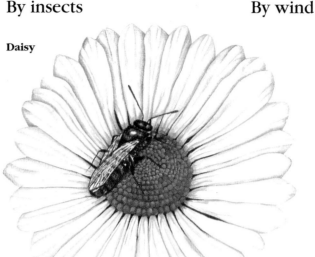

Some flowers make the shape of a platform with their petals for insects to land on easily.

Foxglove

Bees crawl inside some flowers to gather nectar.

By wind

Dog's Mercury

Some plants make it easy for the wind to blow away the pollen. They have a lot of pollen, and the stamens and pistils are not covered.

By itself

Red Helleborine

Some flowers, like the Red Helleborine, can pollinate themselves.

What plants need

Plants need to grow, spread their pollen, and make sure their seeds are scattered far away. To do all these things, they often depend on the weather, the soil and other living creatures - even people.

Some plants need insects to carry pollen.

Plants need the right amount of water and mineral salts in the soil to help them grow.

Plants need certain temperatures, whether they grow in cool or hot places. Most European flowers bloom when it is warm.

Plants need light to make food for themselves and to grow.

How seeds are scattered

Once the seeds have grown in the ovaries, it is important that they are scattered. Then they can begin to grow into another plant. Plants need light to grow, so it is best if they fall away from the parent plant, which might overshadow them and block out the light.

Seeds can be scattered by the wind, by animals and by water. Some plants scatter their seeds by themselves.

By animals

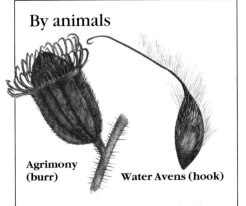

Agrimony (burr) **Water Avens (hook)**

Some seeds have burrs or hooks that stick to animal fur. The seeds eventually drop off the animal and in this way may be carried far from the parent plant.

By wind

Rosebay Willowherb

Seeds with hair "parachutes".

Dandelion ("clock")

Some seeds can float on the wind. Dandelion seeds are inside very small fruits, which have hairs that behave like parachutes.

By water

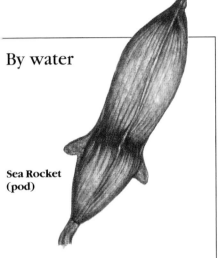

Sea Rocket (pod)

Some seeds are in a pod, like the Sea Rocket pod, that floats in the water until it opens, releasing the seeds.

By explosion

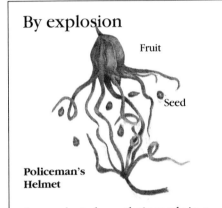

Fruit

Seed

Policeman's Helmet

Some plants have their seeds in a fruit that pops open. The seeds then shoot out, and travel away from the parent plant. The fruits of the Policeman's Helmet do this.

Animals carry seeds and nuts and drop them away from the parent plant.

Some plants need water to carry seeds away from the parent plant.

Birds may fly far from where they eat fruits. The seeds pass through their bodies and fall on the ground.

People often spread seeds without knowing. They get seeds in the soles of their shoes.

Flower record book

You could keep everything you discover about wild flowers in a record book. The best sort of book is a loose-leaf binder, which lets you add pages whenever you wish. This is the perfect place to copy out notes from flower hunting expeditions and keep drawings, maps you have made and photographs.

Everything to do with wild flowers belongs in your book. Record your experiments too. Draw and write about every step of an experiment as it happens.

A flower record book will be a permanent reminder of all the interesting bits of information you discover about the flowers you find.

Common Mallow
Found in a grassy field on July 25th

Stick pressed flowers in your book.

Collecting pictures

Stick magazine pictures or postcards of wild flowers into your book. This way you can add to your record book even in the winter.

Pressing and mounting

Press only a common flower. Place it between two sheets of blotting paper and rest some heavy books on top for about a week.

When it is completely dry, put a dab of glue on the stem. Then fix it carefully to the inside of a clear plastic bag, so you can see both sides.

Stick the bag to a page in your record book with sticky tape. If you know the name of the flower, write it on the page. Write the date and place you found it as well.

Common Fleabane

Found in a damp meadow on August 8th at 11 a.m. 40 cm high 21°C

A simple experiment

Turn a plant away from the light. In a few days time, you will see that the plant is leaning towards the light. Plants grow towards light because they need it to make food. Plants die without light.

Make a collection of flower seeds and pods. Fix them in your book with sticky tape. Remember to label them with their flower's name.

When flowers such as poppies or daises are in bloom, make a list of the insects that visit them. Record this in your notebook.

Drawing and painting

Make coloured drawings or paintings of the quick sketches you did in your notebook when you were outside. Be sure to write down the time of day when you saw the flowers, as plants may look different in the afternoon from in the morning.

Write in your record book any information you can find about customs and festivals where flowers are used.

Leaf rubbing

Put a leaf onto a flat surface with its underside facing you.

Cover it with a piece of thin white paper. Rub backwards and forwards gently over the paper with a crayon or pencil until the shape shows through.

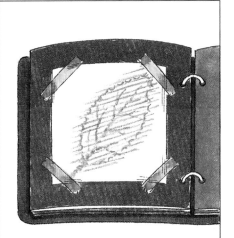

Stick your leaf rubbings into your record book.

Flower calendar

You will find that different plants flower at different times of the year. Make a calendar to help you remember when their flowers appear.

You will also discover that plants change appearance as the seasons change. Draw plants at different stages of their life, first when they are in bud, when the flowers come out and later when the fruits develop.

The pictures of the Arum on the right show how a plant can change its appearance, both inside and out at different stages in its life.

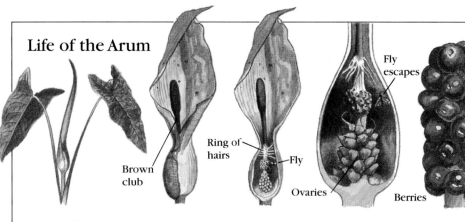

Life of the Arum

Fly escapes · **Ring of hairs** · **Fly** · **Brown club** · **Ovaries** · **Berries**

At first, the Arum is green. When the flower opens, it has a brown club. This attracts flies with its smell, and they get trapped inside the lower part of the flower by a ring of hairs.

The flies drop pollen on the ovaries. Then the hairs wither and the flies escape. In autumn, the ovaries become very poisonous red berries which must never be picked.

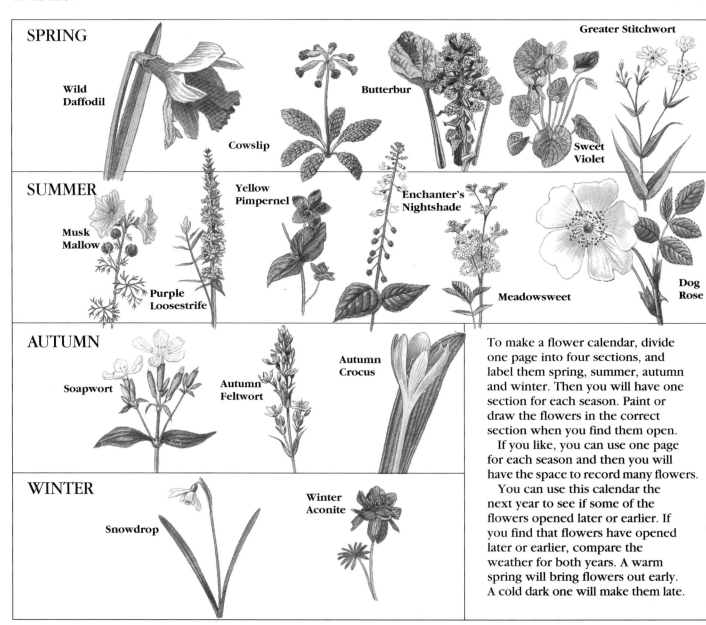

SPRING

Wild Daffodil · Cowslip · Butterbur · Greater Stitchwort · Sweet Violet

SUMMER

Musk Mallow · Purple Loosestrife · Yellow Pimpernel · Enchanter's Nightshade · Meadowsweet · Dog Rose

AUTUMN

Soapwort · Autumn Feltwort · Autumn Crocus

WINTER

Snowdrop · Winter Aconite

To make a flower calendar, divide one page into four sections, and label them spring, summer, autumn and winter. Then you will have one section for each season. Paint or draw the flowers in the correct section when you find them open.

If you like, you can use one page for each season and then you will have the space to record many flowers.

You can use this calendar the next year to see if some of the flowers opened later or earlier. If you find that flowers have opened later or earlier, compare the weather for both years. A warm spring will bring flowers out early. A cold dark one will make them late.

Rivers and ponds

Look for plants in different places around fresh water. If they actually grow in the water, they may be rooted to the bottom or their roots may float freely. Their leaves may be under the water or floating on top of it. If plants are growing on land, they may be at the water's edge, on the banks, or in swamps. Most water plants have their flowers above the water. They are usually pollinated by insects or wind, not by water.

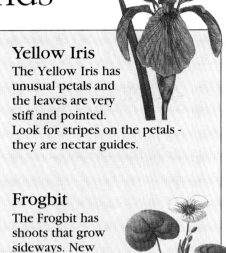

Yellow Iris
The Yellow Iris has unusual petals and the leaves are very stiff and pointed. Look for stripes on the petals - they are nectar guides.

Frogbit
The Frogbit has shoots that grow sideways. New plants grow upwards from these shoots.

Duckweed
Duckweed can grow to cover a whole pond. It floats on top of still water.

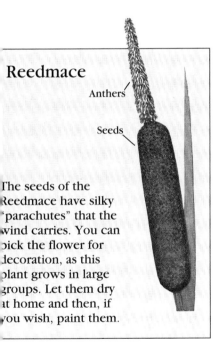

Reedmace

Anthers

Seeds

The seeds of the Reedmace have silky "parachutes" that the wind carries. You can pick the flower for decoration, as this plant grows in large groups. Let them dry at home and then, if you wish, paint them.

Water Lily
The petals of the Water Lily give shade to pond creatures in hot weather. They can rest on the broad, thick leaves.

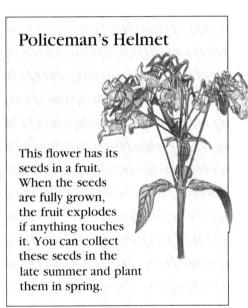

Policeman's Helmet
This flower has its seeds in a fruit. When the seeds are fully grown, the fruit explodes if anything touches it. You can collect these seeds in the late summer and plant them in spring.

The leaves of fresh-water plants

The leaves of plants growing in fresh water can be all shapes and sizes - oval, round, short or long. This is because some grow under the water's surface and some on top of it, and the water itself can be still or fast-moving.

The Water Crowfoot has broad leaves above the water and thread-like leaves below the water. The Water Soldier floats completely below the water's surface.

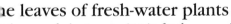
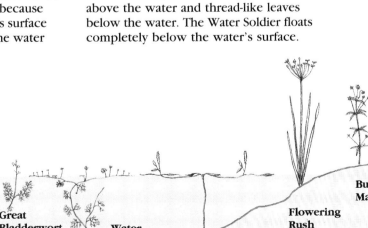
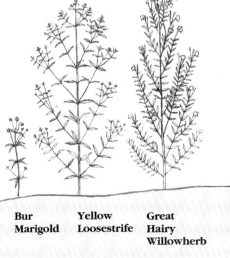

Spiked Water Milfoil

Water Soldier

Great Bladderwort

Water Crowfoot

Amphibious Bistort

Flowering Rush

Bur Marigold

Yellow Loosestrife

Great Hairy Willowherb

Fields, meadows and marshes

Some fields are used for animals to graze in and others for growing crops such as wheat and barley. You will see different flowers in different kinds of fields.

Grass grows in meadows and this is often cut to make hay. Marshes are grassy areas that are waterlogged all or almost all of the time. The flowers you find in a meadow will often be different from those you find in a marsh.

Wet soil is rich in many things that plants need to grow. This means you will find a lot of flowers in wet areas.

Marsh Marigold

This flower grows in wet meadows and looks like a large, thick-petalled buttercup.

Meadow Clary

This flower is quite common. It can be confused with Wild Clary, which has more jagged leaves and is more rare.

Marsh Thistle
The flowers are in clusters. There are prickly leaves on the dark green stems.

Yellow Rattle
When the wind blows the ripe seeds rattle inside their fruits.

Common Comfrey
The flowers are bell-shaped and hang down. You can make tea from the leaves.

Red Clover
The flower heads are made up of dozens of sweet-smelling flowers.

Wild Pansy
The flowers are violet or yellow, or a mixture of both colours.

Marsh Orchid
This plant has very unusual pink flowers. You should never pick it, or dig up the roots, as it is quite rare.

It is important to notice where flowers are growing when you find them. Marsh Orchids, for example, will often be found in the shade of a tree. Write in your notebook as many facts as possible, such as how wet or dry the soil was, if a stream was nearby, or if the land was being used for a crop or grazing animals. Often the position of a flower can be a great help when trying to identify it.

Fruit

Creeping Buttercup
This plant has creeping stems which root easily.

Water Avens
The sepals and petals are both red, and the flowers hang in a nodding position. The fruits are easy to spot.

Meadowsweet
The flowers are in clusters and smell sweet to attract insects.

Creeping Jenny
The flowers are bell-shaped and the creeping stems are matted on the ground.

Common Valerian
These red-pink flowers are common near water. They smell very unpleasant. The stem is quite stout.

Water Forget-me-Not
This plant grows near water. It is covered in soft hairs and the flower has a yellow centre.

Hedgerows and roadsides

A hedgerow is a line of specially planted bushes, usually along the edges of fields. Often other bushes start to grow in between the planted ones to give a mixture of plants. Hedgerows are important because many flowers, such as Cow Parsley, grow alongside them. As fields are cultivated and meadows mown for hay, hedgerows are often the only place left where flowers can live and grow. This means that when hedgerows are destroyed, the flowers near them usually die.

Hedgerows give shade and shelter to flowers. Often seeds are blown into a hedge and get trapped. Later they fall to the ground and start to grow.

Flowers growing on grassy verges at the roadside must be tough and strong to survive car exhaust fumes and the litter dumped on them.

Wild Clematis
The fruits have long white hairs.

Dog Rose
Birds eat the red fruits, called rosehips.

Cow Parsley
The flowers make a landing platform for insects.

Honeysuckle
The flowers are pollinated at night by moths.

Stinging Nettle
There are stinging hairs on the leaves. The flowers are green.

Greater Burdock
The fruits stick to the fur of animals.

Dandelion
The seeds form a feathery "clock", a float away when you blow them.

Foxglove
These flowers are very poisonous. Do not touch them.

Common Teasel
In winter, Common Teasels are brown and brittle.

Fruit

Seeds

Herb Robert

Look for the fruit of the Herb Robert. When the seeds are fully grown, the fruit explodes, and the seeds shoot out.

Stinging Nettle

Tortoiseshell Butterfly

The small Tortoiseshell Butterfly lays its eggs on the leaves of the Stinging Nettle. If you find any eggs, do not touch them.

Dog Rose

Wild Clematis

Honeysuckle

Wild Clematis and Honeysuckle wrap themselves around the Dog Rose. This rose has hook-like thorns to help it climb.

Make a scent jar

Make a scent jar from any flower petals that have a nice smell, such as Honeysuckle or Wild Strawberry. Put the petals between two sheets of blotting paper (picture 1) and press them under a pile of books for about a week, or until they are dry. Put the dried petals in a jar with some pieces of dried orange or lemon peel, and a bay leaf. Prepare the lid of your scent jar by punching holes with a pencil in a circle of tin foil (picture 2). Fix the foil lid carefully over and fasten it with

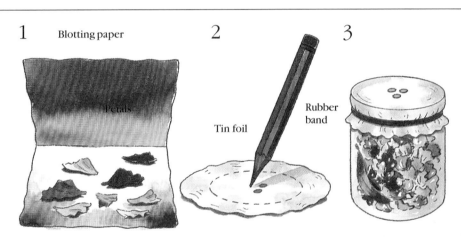

1 Blotting paper

Petals

2 Tin foil

3 Rubber band

a rubber band (picture 3).
   You can also put the petals in little bags that you have sewn out of fabric.

Leave one side of the bag open until you have put the dried petals inside. Then sew it up completely.

Creeping Cinquefoil
The creeping stems are called runners.

Greater Stitchwort
The delicate stem is square, not round.

Herb Robert
The flowers droop at night or in bad weather.

Wild Strawberry
The flowers have a nice scent.

Bird's-foot Trefoil

Coltsfoot
The seeds form a feathery "clock" like the Dandelion's.

19

Woodlands

In the summer and autumn, when all the trees are in full leaf, you will probably find only a few flowers on the ground beneath them. This is because the leaves are blocking the sunlight from reaching the flowers. The time when you usually find a lot of flowers in woodlands is in spring before the leaves have come out on the trees. Another reason for not seeing many flowers in woods is that the roots of trees take almost all the food from the soil. The kinds of flowers you will find change with the type of trees growing and the season.

At the edge of woods there will be more flowers because there is more sunlight. See for yourself how many grow near the edge and how many where it is very shady.

Primrose
A pale yellow flower, it blooms early in the year before the leaves come out on the trees.

Dog's Mercury
It often carpets the ground and is very poisonous.

Oak tree in winter

Oak leaf

Acorn

Oak woods

The top picture shows an oak wood. When oak trees grow big, very little light filters down through their leaves. Even grasses find it hard to grow. A good place to hunt for flowers in an oak wood is near a path at the edge of the wood.

Beech woods

The bottom picture shows a beech wood. Beech trees grow best where the soil does not hold much water. The flowers in beech woods also prefer soil that is not too wet. See if the flowers you find in a beech wood are different from those in an oak wood.

Note

In these pictures we have left out some of the trees so you can see the flowers. In real woodlands the trees would be closer together. The scenes here are like those on the edge of woodland. Many flowers here appear before the leaves are fully out on the trees.

Bluebell
Each flower is bell-shaped and sweet-scented.

Sweet Woodruff
The stems are square not round.

Beech tree in winter

Beech leaf

Beech nut

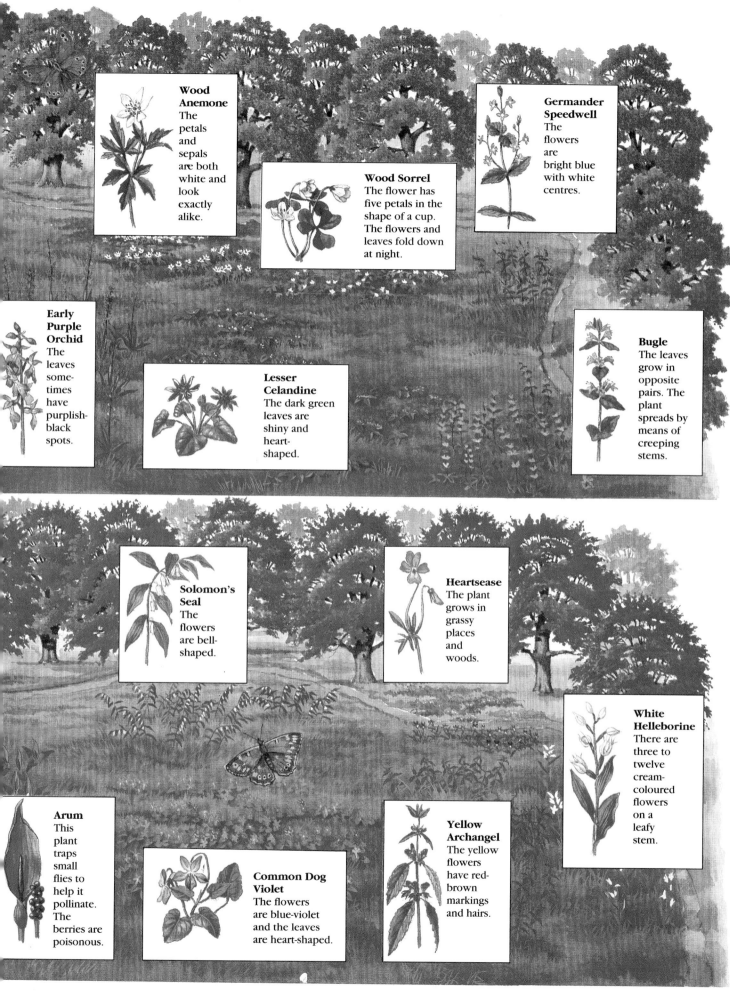

Wood Anemone
The petals and sepals are both white and look exactly alike.

Wood Sorrel
The flower has five petals in the shape of a cup. The flowers and leaves fold down at night.

Germander Speedwell
The flowers are bright blue with white centres.

Early Purple Orchid
The leaves sometimes have purplish-black spots.

Lesser Celandine
The dark green leaves are shiny and heart-shaped.

Bugle
The leaves grow in opposite pairs. The plant spreads by means of creeping stems.

Solomon's Seal
The flowers are bell-shaped.

Heartsease
The plant grows in grassy places and woods.

White Helleborine
There are three to twelve cream-coloured flowers on a leafy stem.

Arum
This plant traps small flies to help it pollinate. The berries are poisonous.

Common Dog Violet
The flowers are blue-violet and the leaves are heart-shaped.

Yellow Archangel
The yellow flowers have red-brown markings and hairs.

21

The seashore

Plants near the seashore must survive in very difficult conditions. The hot sun can dry them out very quickly. Strong winds can dry them out too or blow them over.

They must find ways of not losing the water inside them. To stop water escaping, some plants have a thick outer layer to trap the water, while others have a waxy coat over their leaves, or roll up their leaves when it is very hot and sunny.

Other plants may have small leaves, hairs on their leaves which shield them from the sun, or grow spines instead of leaves.

Plants must be sturdy enough not to blow over in the strong sea winds. This means they either have strong deep roots clinging onto mud, stones and rocks, or grow close to the ground so that there is less chance of them blowing over.

Salt marshes

Salt marshes are made of sand and mud. Be careful when you walk there. It is very easy to sink in. Go with a friend and wear rubber boots. The land in such places has slowly taken over from the sea. That is why the soil is salty.

There are different sections in salt marshes, called zones. Different plants grow in different zones. Many plants that grow in salt marshes do not grow further inland.

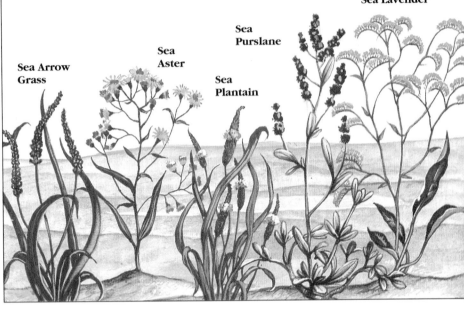

Sand dunes

Like salt marshes, sand dunes have different zones. The types of plants in each zone change according to how near the zone is to the sea and how much the dunes have been held together by plants such as Marram Grass. Couch Grass will be in a zone nearer to the sea than Ragwort.

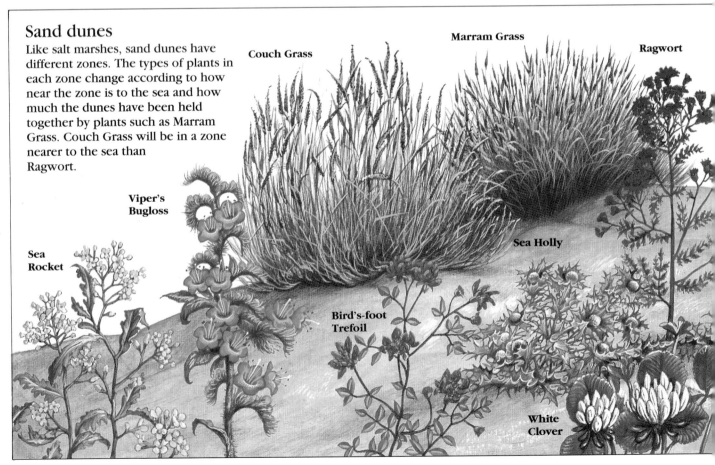

Shingle Beaches

Not many plants can grow here. These beaches are made of pebbles that once were part of cliffs or rocks. The pebbles have been worn down by the pounding of the sea. There is some sand mixed in with the pebbles, and in many places the shingle is constantly on the move. Only plants with deep roots, such as the Yellow Horned Poppy and the Sea Pea, can anchor themselves firmly enough to survive in the shingle.

Shrubby Seablite

Yellow Horned Poppy

Sea pea

Sea Bindweed

Cliffs

Plants struggle to grow here. The winds can be very fierce and blow a lot of the time. Small plants whose roots are not deep can be torn up. The rainwater drains away very quickly, leaving little for the plants. There is almost no soil. Plants must send their roots deep into cracks in the rock. Sometimes they grow along the steep sides of a cliff and can be sprayed with salty water from the sea.

Cliffs may have more soil at the top and there you may be able to find some land plants. Be careful when you look at flowers there. Do not climb any cliffs, and keep well back from the edge.

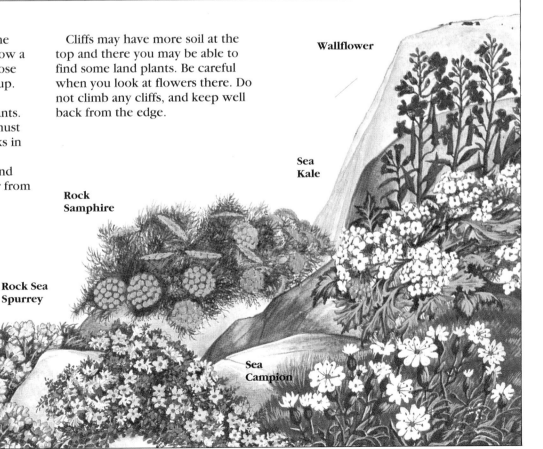

Wallflower

Sea Kale

Rock Samphire

Rock Sea Spurrey

Thrift

Sea Campion

Cities and towns

Flowers grow in waste lands, streets, car parks, gardens, on walls, or any other place in towns and cities where they can find enough soil.

Many flowers can spread quickly over open ground. Some of these flowers are called weeds. Weeds are often stronger than the plants people grow in their gardens, and they can take over. This is a big problem for gardeners.

The flowers in this section are not drawn to scale.

Seed experiment

Heat some soil in an old pan in the oven for about an hour. This will kill any seeds in the soil. Put the pan outside. After a while do wild flowers start to grow? If so, how do you think they get there?

Wallflower
This is a garden flower, but it often "escapes" and can survive from year to year in the wild.

Pellitory of the Wall
This plant looks rather like a Stinging Nettle, but it has no stinging hairs. The stem is reddish-brown.

Prickly Sow Thistle
The leaves are spiny and clasp the stem. The flowers are pale yellow, about 2.5 cm across.

Ivy-leaved Toadflax
The plant is delicate and trailing, with tiny purple flowers, which have curved spurs. The stems are weak.

Dandelion
There is one flower head, made up of many tiny flowers, on each hollow stalk, which contains a milky juice.

Shepherd's Purse
A common weed in cities and towns. The seeds are held in a heart-shaped fruit. Flowers are white.

Ribwort Plantain
The flowers grow on small dark brown spikes. The anthers are pale yellow or purple.

White Clover
The leaves have three (and very rarely four) leaflets. The white flowers have a sweet smell to attract insects.

Golden Rod
The bright yellow flower heads are made up of dozens of tiny flowers. The seeds have hair parachutes.

Evening Primrose
This flower came originally from America and now grows wild in all parts of Europe.

Common Toadflax
Each flower has an orange spot on the lower lip and a spur (a horn-shaped tube growing from a petal).

Wall Pennywort
Look for the circular leaves on stalks - they are like tiny umbrellas. The flowers are tube-shaped.

Oxford Ragwort
The leaves have "teeth" and the flower heads grow in groups. The plant grows on bare or waste ground.

Rosebay Willowherb
The flowers have four bright pink petals, and the seeds have silky white hairs. They bloom from June to September.

White Campion
This flower is pollinated by moths at night, and the plant has sticky hairs on it.

Daisy
One of the commonest European flowers. It also grows in short grass in fields. The flowers close up at night.

Wild Chamomile
The plant spreads over wide areas, and has a nice smell when crushed. The petals may point down.

Moors and mountains

Moors

Moors are open lands that are swept by wind. Heathland is very similar. Some of these areas are very dry and some are waterlogged from time to time. Water collects in poor soil, such as in high land or near the coast. You will find fewer flowers on moors and heaths than in meadows and fields. The ones that do grow sometimes take over large sections of land.

Different flowers grow on different types of moors and heaths. The most common moorland plant is Common Heather. Sometimes it is burnt to encourage new shoots to grow. The Common Gorse is very widespread on heaths.

Alpine Bearberry
The plant has small white flowers and grows low on the ground. The unripe berries are red, and later turn blue.

Bilberry
The plant is bushy, with blue-black berries and red flowers.

Sheep's Bit
The soft blue flowers are in a rounded head and the leaves are narrow. The plant is slightly hairy.

Bog Moss
Areas covered in Bog Moss can be very wet and unsafe to walk on.

Mountains

The seeds of mountain flowers find it difficult to grow in the poor soils and the cold, windy weather of mountains. The higher up a mountain you go, the fewer flowers you will find. Trees cannot grow high up on a mountain because of the strong winds and lack of soil.

Some plants can grow high up on a mountain-side. They grow low so that the strong winds will not blow them away. Many mountain flowers spread by sending out creeping stems, which root.

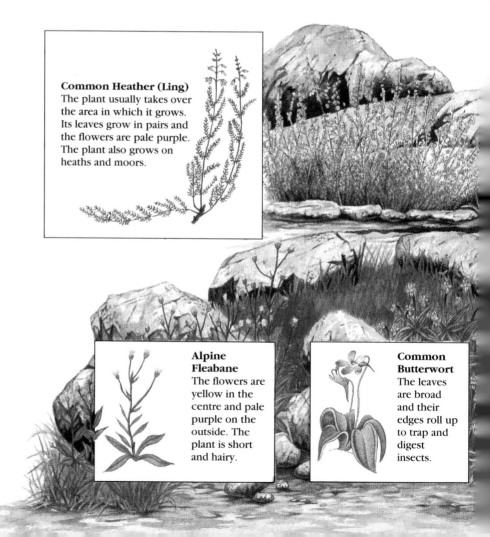

Common Heather (Ling)
The plant usually takes over the area in which it grows. Its leaves grow in pairs and the flowers are pale purple. The plant also grows on heaths and moors.

Alpine Fleabane
The flowers are yellow in the centre and pale purple on the outside. The plant is short and hairy.

Common Butterwort
The leaves are broad and their edges roll up to trap and digest insects.

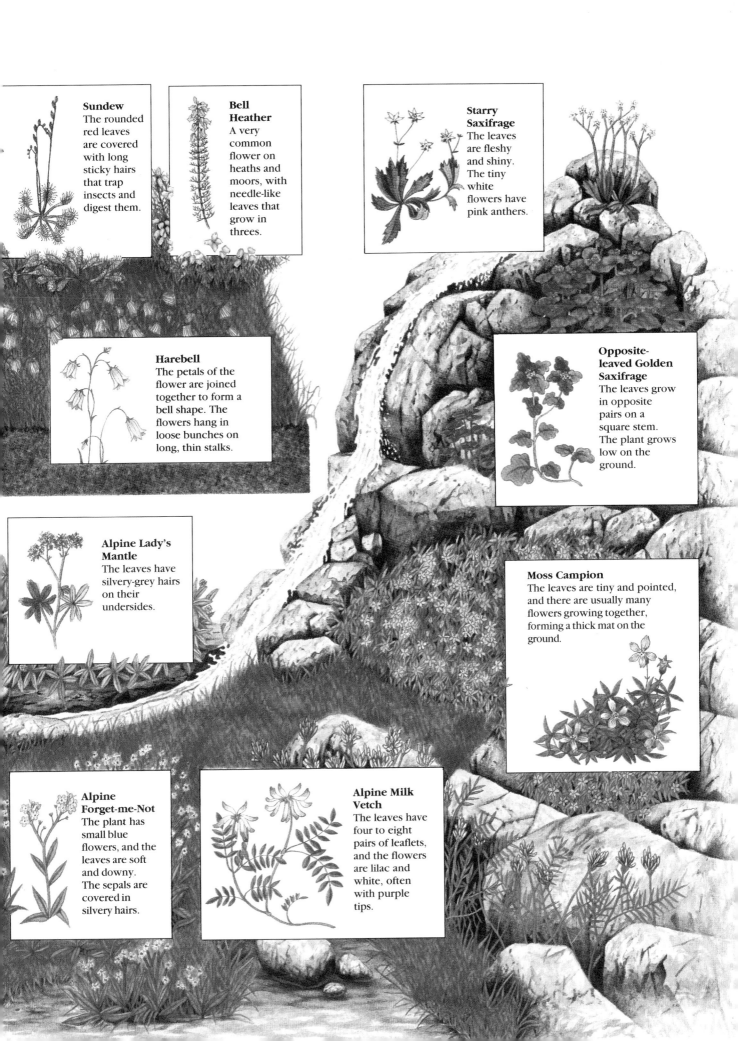

Sundew
The rounded red leaves are covered with long sticky hairs that trap insects and digest them.

Bell Heather
A very common flower on heaths and moors, with needle-like leaves that grow in threes.

Starry Saxifrage
The leaves are fleshy and shiny. The tiny white flowers have pink anthers.

Harebell
The petals of the flower are joined together to form a bell shape. The flowers hang in loose bunches on long, thin stalks.

Opposite-leaved Golden Saxifrage
The leaves grow in opposite pairs on a square stem. The plant grows low on the ground.

Alpine Lady's Mantle
The leaves have silvery-grey hairs on their undersides.

Moss Campion
The leaves are tiny and pointed, and there are usually many flowers growing together, forming a thick mat on the ground.

Alpine Forget-me-Not
The plant has small blue flowers, and the leaves are soft and downy. The sepals are covered in silvery hairs.

Alpine Milk Vetch
The leaves have four to eight pairs of leaflets, and the flowers are lilac and white, often with purple tips.

Identifying flowers by colour

White flowers

Fruit (pod)

Fruit

Field Pennycress
30 cm. Waste ground.
Flowers in summer.

Sea Rocket
30 cm. Sandy coasts.
Flowers in summer.

Bladder Campion
45 cm. Waste ground,
grassy places. Flowers
in spring/summer.

Greater Stitchwort
20 cm. Woods, hedges,
fields. Flowers in
spring.

Star-of-Bethlehem
15 cm. Grassy places.
Flowers in early
summer.

Cloudberry
15 cm. Upland bogs,
damp moors. Flowers
in summer.

White Stonecrop
Low and creeping. Rocks,
walls. Flowers in summer.

White Bryony
Climbs to 4 m. Hedges,
scrub. Flowers in
spring/summer.

White Dead Nettle
20 cm. Waysides,
waste places.
Flowers spring to
autumn.

Feverfew
30 cm. Walls,
waste places.
Flowers in summer.

Flower

Cow Parsley
60 cm. Hedge-banks,
shady places.
Flowers in spring.

Flower

Flower

White Melilot
60 cm. Bare and
waste ground.
Flowers in summer.

Hogweed
Up to 3 m. Grassy places,
open woods. Flowers
spring to autumn.

Flower

Daisy
10 cm. Lawns,
short grass, fields.
Flowers all year.

Yarrow
30 cm. Grassy
places. Flowers in
summer/autumn.

Flower

28 **In these sections on colour, you will find the average height of the plant from ground level to the top, the season when the plant comes into flower, and the place where it is most likely to be found.**

llow flowers

Bulbous Buttercup
5 cm. Grassland.
Flowers in spring.

Marsh Marigold
15 cm. Wet places.
Flowers in spring/
summer.

Yellow Horned Poppy
60 cm. Sea shingle,
waste places inland.
Flowers in summer.

Monkey Flower
20 cm. Wet
places. Flowers
in summer.

Yellow Rattle
30 cm. Grassy places,
and fields. Flowers
in spring/summer.

Flower

Wild Cabbage
60 cm. Sea cliffs.
Flowers in summer.

Silverweed
Low, creeping. Damp
grassy places. Flowers
in spring/summer.

Lady's Bedstraw
10 cm. Dry, grassy
places. Flowers
in summer.

Yellow Chamomile
30 cm. Dry, bare
and waste places.
Flowers in summer.

Groundsel
10 cm. Gardens
and waste ground.
Flowers all year.

Flower

Common Gorse
Up to 2.5 m. Heaths,
grassland.
Flowers all year.

Common Rockrose
Close to the ground.
Grassy and rocky places.
Flowers in summer.

Kidney Vetch
15 cm. Dry grassland,
by sea, mountains.
Flowers spring/summer.

**Perforate St John's
Wort**
45 cm. Grassy places.
Flowers in summer.

Yellow Water Lily
4 cm above water. Still
water, slow streams.
Flowers in summer.

**Remember - if you cannot see a picture of the flower you want to identify here, look in the sections earlier in the book which link
flowers with the places where they grow.**

Pink and red flowers

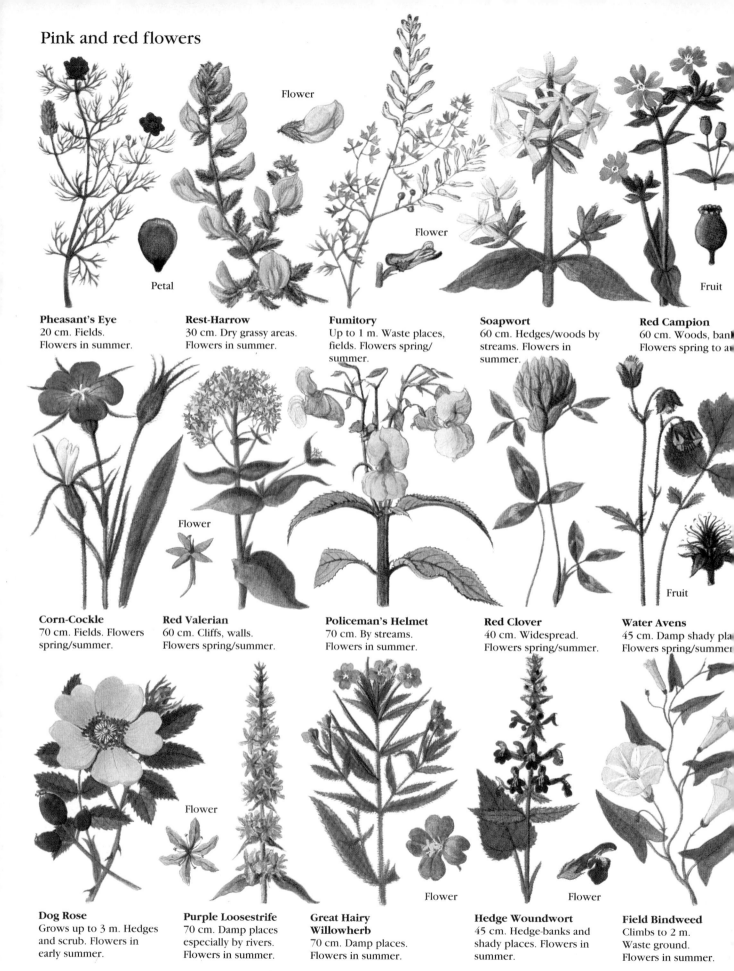

Flower

Petal

Flower

Flower

Fruit

Pheasant's Eye
20 cm. Fields.
Flowers in summer.

Rest-Harrow
30 cm. Dry grassy areas.
Flowers in summer.

Fumitory
Up to 1 m. Waste places,
fields. Flowers spring/
summer.

Soapwort
60 cm. Hedges/woods by
streams. Flowers in
summer.

Red Campion
60 cm. Woods, ban
Flowers spring to a

Flower

Fruit

Corn-Cockle
70 cm. Fields. Flowers
spring/summer.

Red Valerian
60 cm. Cliffs, walls.
Flowers spring/summer.

Policeman's Helmet
70 cm. By streams.
Flowers in summer.

Red Clover
40 cm. Widespread.
Flowers spring/summer.

Water Avens
45 cm. Damp shady pla
Flowers spring/summer

Flower

Flower

Flower

Dog Rose
Grows up to 3 m. Hedges
and scrub. Flowers in
early summer.

Purple Loosestrife
70 cm. Damp places
especially by rivers.
Flowers in summer.

**Great Hairy
Willowherb**
70 cm. Damp places.
Flowers in summer.

Hedge Woundwort
45 cm. Hedge-banks and
shady places. Flowers in
summer.

Field Bindweed
Climbs to 2 m.
Waste ground.
Flowers in summer.

In these sections on colour, you will find the average height of the plant from ground level to the top, the season when the
plant comes into flower, and the place where it is most likely to be found.

Blue and mauve flowers

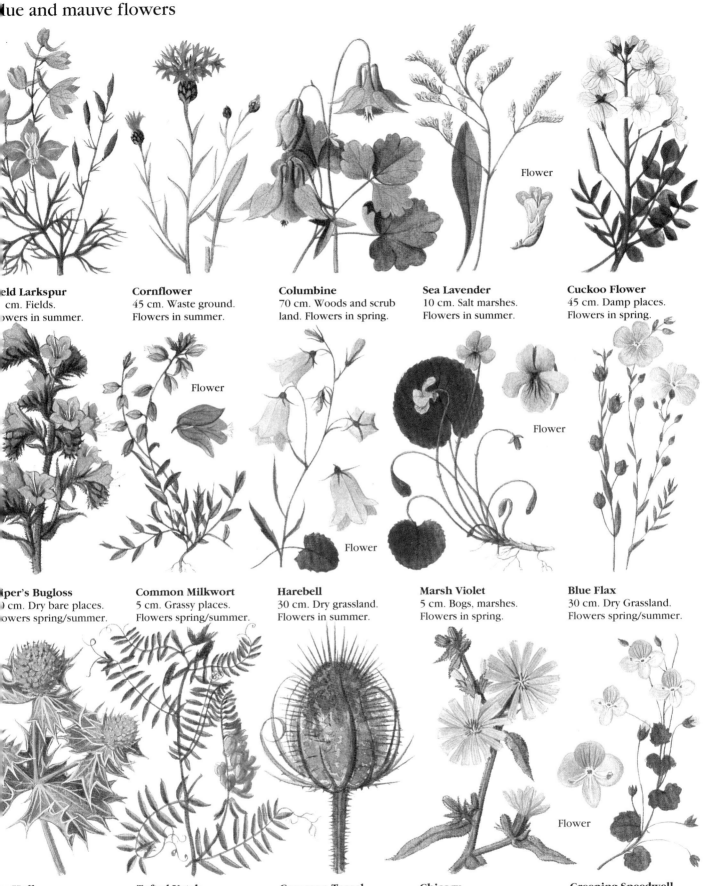

Field Larkspur
cm. Fields.
owers in summer.

Cornflower
45 cm. Waste ground.
Flowers in summer.

Columbine
70 cm. Woods and scrub
land. Flowers in spring.

Sea Lavender
10 cm. Salt marshes.
Flowers in summer.

Flower

Cuckoo Flower
45 cm. Damp places.
Flowers in spring.

Flower

Flower

Flower

per's Bugloss
cm. Dry bare places.
owers spring/summer.

Common Milkwort
5 cm. Grassy places.
Flowers spring/summer.

Harebell
30 cm. Dry grassland.
Flowers in summer.

Marsh Violet
5 cm. Bogs, marshes.
Flowers in spring.

Blue Flax
30 cm. Dry Grassland.
Flowers spring/summer.

Flower

a Holly
cm. By the sea on
nd and shingle.
wers in summer.

Tufted Vetch
Climbs to 1.5 m.
Hedges and bushy places.
Flowers in summer.

Common Teasel
70 cm. Grassy and
bushy places.
Flowers in summer.

Chicory
60 cm. Grassy and
waste places.
Flowers in summer.

Creeping Speedwell
Low. Lawns and
grassy places.
Flowers in spring.

member - if you cannot see a picture of the flower you want to identify here, look in the sections earlier in the book which link
wers with the places where they grow.

Index

Books to Read

The Observer's Book of Wild Flowers. W
  J. Stokoe (Warne)
Collins' Photoguide to Wild Flowers. Oleg
  Polunin (Collins)
The Wild Flowers of Britain and Northern
  Europe. R. Fitter, A. Fitter, M. Blamey
  (Collins)
Country Diary of Creating a Wild Flower
  Garden. J. Andrews (Webb and Bower)

Clubs to join

The Council for Environmental Conservation (address: 80 York Way, London N1 9AG) will supply the addresses of your local **Natural History Societies**. Send an S.A.E. for the list. Many of these have specialist sections and almost all have field meetings. **The Royal Society for Nature Conservation** (address: Vigilant House, 120 Wilton Road, London SW1V 1J2) will give you the address of your local **County Naturalist Trust**, which may have a junior branch. Many of the Trusts have meetings and lectures, and offer opportunities for work on nature reserves.

National organizations

The Botanical Society of the British Isles, c/o Natural History Museum, Cromwell Road, London SW7 5BD.
English Nature, Northminster House, Northminster Road, Peterborough PE1 1UA.
The Countryside Commission, John Dower House, Crescent Place, Cheltenham, Gloucestershire GL5O 3RA.
The Biological Records Centre (address: Monks Wood Experimental Station, Abbots Ripton, Cambs PE17 2LS) co-ordinates survey work of people throughout Britain, to make records of changes in the countryside.